Simple Machines

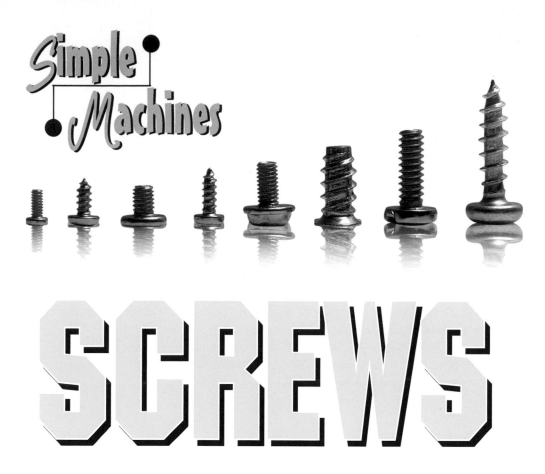

SCREWS

Authors: David and Patricia Armentrout

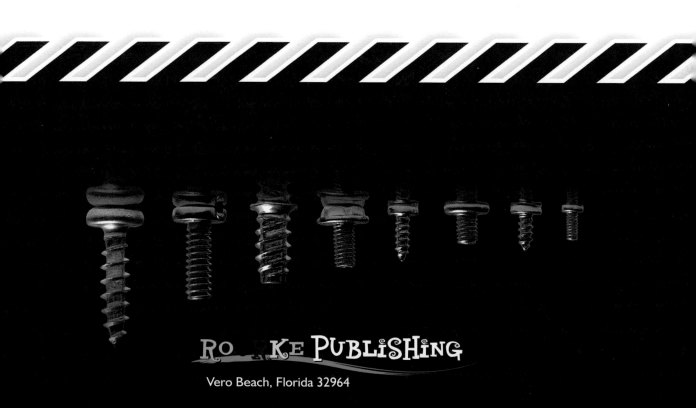

ROURKE PUBLISHING

Vero Beach, Florida 32964

www.rourkepublishing.com

PHOTO CREDITS: © brightstorm: Title page; © robcocquyt: page 05; © Kokhanchikov: page 07; © Serge Lamere: page 08; © Gregory Donald Horler: page 09; © Vasilius: page 10; © Armentrout: page 11; © Adam Gryko: page 13; © Armentrout: page 14; © Armentrout: page 15; © Terrie L. Zeller: page 16; © PictureQuest: page 17; © Armentrout: page 19; © Despot: page 20; © Bernd Jürgens: page 21; © Lincoln Rogers: page 22

Edited by Kelli L. Hicks

Cover and Interior designed by Tara Raymo

Library of Congress Cataloging-in-Publication Data

Armentrout, David, 1962-
  Screws / David and Patricia Armentrout.
     p. cm. -- (Simple machines)
  Previous ed. by Patricia Armentrout under title: Screw.
  ISBN 978-1-60694-390-8
  1. Screws--Juvenile literature. I. Armentrout, Patricia, 1960- II.
Armentrout, Patricia, 1960- Screw. III. Title.
  TJ1338.A76 2010
  621.8'82--dc22
                              2009006075

www.rourkepublishing.com – rourke@rourkepublishing.com
Post Office Box 643328 Vero Beach, Florida 32964

TABLE OF CONTENTS

MACHINES

Have you ever watched someone cut down a tree, repair a roof, or build a tree house? If so, you probably noticed they used tools like axes, hammers, and drills.

Imagine driving a nail without a hammer, or splitting a tree trunk without an axe. Those tasks would be difficult without tools. That is because tools are machines. Machines make our work easier.

A hammer and nails are both simple machines. The force from the swing of the hammer forces the nail into the wood.

Think about how our modern lifestyle depends on machines. Farmers use tractors to plant and harvest crops. Automakers use robots to assemble cars. Construction crews use cranes and other heavy equipment to build bridges and buildings. The machines they use are **complex**; they have many moving parts.

Before the invention of complex machines, people used simple machines. They include the wheel, pulley, lever, wedge, inclined plane, and screw. We still use them today. In fact, without simple machines, there would be no complex machines.

A motorized tiller is a complex machine that helps make the difficult task of turning the soil to prepare a garden for planting a little easier.

SIMPLE MACHINES

Simple machines are basic, but they are very useful. Wheels help us move things with less **friction**. We use pulleys and levers to lift or move heavy objects. Wedges help us split things apart. Inclined planes, or slopes, help us get from one level to the next.

Screws help us do many different jobs. They are unusual, and have a funny shape. But, it's their shape that makes them so useful. Let's explore how.

You have to be careful not to use too much force when working with a chisel or you could damage the surface of your project.

If you want to go ice fishing, you might use a simple machine called a hand ice auger to drill holes in the ice.

SCREWS

Screws are available in different sizes, shapes, and materials. Most are metal, but some screws are wood, or even plastic. Some are long and thin, others are short and fat.

Most screws have three parts: a rounded or flat top, a pointed or flat bottom, and a shaft in the middle with a thread that winds around it.

Bottom

Shaft

Top

Screws are like nails because we use them to hold two or more objects together.

The advantage that screws have over nails is that objects can be held together and taken apart over and over again without damaging the screw or the objects.

What makes a screw so useful? The spiraling thread is its secret weapon. It has a sharp edge. As a screw spirals through wood, for instance, the thread cuts a groove. The groove is a path for the rest of the thread to follow. Each turn pulls the screw deeper into the wood. The screw comes to a stop when the head meets the surface of the wood.

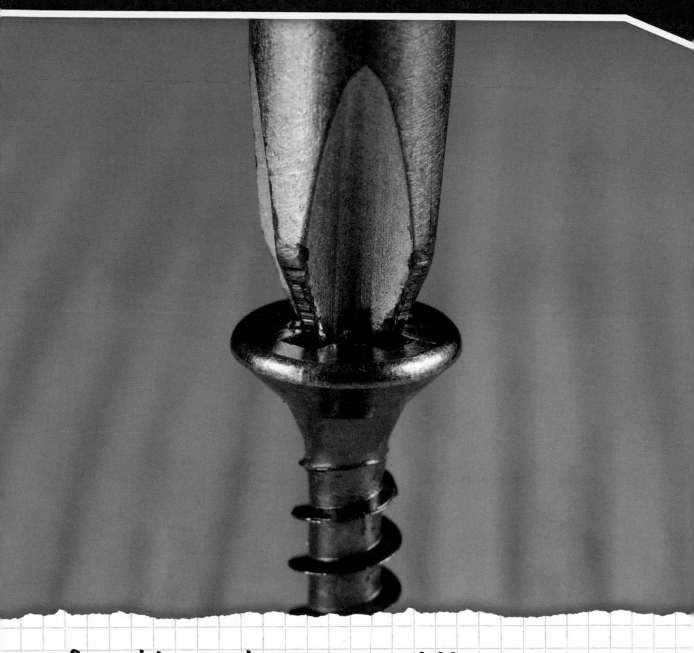

Screwdrivers and screws are available in many different sizes. Turn this Phillips screwdriver clockwise to hold two objects together. To unscrew objects held together by a screw, you turn the screwdriver counterclockwise.

THAT'S SCREWY

The screw is actually an inclined plane wrapped around a shaft. Use a square piece of paper and a colored marker to see how.

Fold the paper diagonally to form a triangle. With the marker, color a line along the fold. Use a different edge as the bottom and hold it over a table. The colored edge forms an inclined plane, or slope. Now, put the triangle colored side down on the table. Lay the marker on one of the short sides and roll it up tightly. Stand the marker up. Do you see a colorful thread spiraling up a shaft?

Performing an experiment at home is a fun way
of testing your scientific knowledge and seeing
for yourself how simple machines work.

CAN YOU DIG IT?

Did you know we use screws when we drill holes? Drills hold screw-shaped bits that spin. The bits **bore** holes through wood, metal, and other materials. We use small hand drills for simple projects like hanging window blinds and curtain rods. However, we need big drilling machines to tackle tough jobs. Oil workers use giant bits to drill for oil. Engineers carve tunnels with powerful boring machines. Their special screws cut away dirt and rock.

Drill

Threads —— Drill Bit

Drill bits have sharp cutting threads.

SCREWS THAT SEAL

Screws are helpful, even when they do not bore holes. Some screws form a tight seal. To find a good example, look in your refrigerator or pantry for a jar. Any kind of jar will do, as long as it has a screw-on lid. Open the jar and look inside the lid. Do you see the grooves? Now, notice the thread on the lip of the jar. The thread fits between the grooves on the lid. When you screw on the lid, the thread follows the groove and forms a tight seal.

You use a simple machine
when you open a screw-top water bottle.

SCREWS THAT MOVE

Some machines use the screw to move air or water. Consider a fan. A fan feels nice on a hot summer day. Spinning blades pull air from behind them and push it out the other side. The breeze cools you off. Boat propellers are screws too, but they move water instead of air. The moving water propels boats forward.

Farmers even use the screw to move solids like corn and wheat. Harvesting machines have a giant screw, or **auger**, that moves grain. The spinning auger's giant thread directs freshly cut grain into neat piles, or onto a moving belt. The belt dumps the grain into a holding tank.

AUGER

Farmers once used animals pulling a plow to harvest crops, but they now have machines to help finish the work faster.

MAKING WORK EASIER

Simple machines, like screws, are important. They help us get work done with less effort. Some jobs would be impossible without them.

When you see people working, notice the different types of machines they use. Can you see how simple machines make their work easier?

Snow blowers use augers to move fresh snow.

GLOSSARY

auger (AW-gur): a spinning tool that bores holes or moves material

bore (BOR): to make a hole with a tool that rotates

complex (KAHM-pleks): made up of many parts

friction (FRIK-shun): a force that slows two objects when they rub together

lever (LEV-ur): a strong, rigid bar that rests or pivots on a support used to lift and move objects

INDEX

WEBSITES TO VISIT

www.kidskonnect.com/content/view/99/27

www.edheads.org/activities/simple-machines

www.brainpop.com/technology/simplemachines

ABOUT THE AUTHORS

David and Patricia Armentrout specialize in nonfiction children's books. They enjoy exploring different topics, and have written on a variety of subjects, including communities, sports, animals, and people. David and Patricia love to spend their free time outdoors with their two boys and dog Max.